W9-BEN-348

WITHDRAWN

Artisans Around the World

Northern Asia

Mary Tull, Tristan Franklin, and Cynthia A. Black

RSVP

RAINTREE
STECK-VAUGHN
P U B L I S H E R S
A Steck-Vaughn Company

Austin, Texas

www.steck-vaughn.com

Developed by Franklin Tull, Inc.,
Manager: Sharon Franklin
Designer: Dahna Solar
Maps: Terragraphics, Inc.
Illustrators: Dahna Solar and James Cloutier
Picture Researcher: Mary Tull
Projects: Cynthia A. Black

Raintree Steck-Vaughn Publishers Staff
Project Manager: Joyce Spicer
Editor: Pam Wells
Electronic Production: Scott Melcer

Photo Credits: Gary Tepfer: pp. 8UL, 8LL, 8LR, 9UR, 9L, 10UL, 10UR, 10L, 11UR, 12UL, 12UR; Phyllis Barkhurst: p. 8UR; Vince Streano/
The Stock Solution: p. 16UL; Korean Overseas Information Service-Korean Cultural Center of Los Angeles: pp. 16UR, 16LL, 16LR, 17UR, 17L,
18UL, 19UR, 19LL, 20UR, 20LL; Jim Shipee/Unicorn Stock Photos: p18UR; Florent Flipper/Unicorn Stock Photos: p. 24UL; Carl Purcell/
The Stock Solution: pp. 24LR, 28UR, 34LR; ©Ru Suichu/ChinaStock: p. 24LL; Bachmann/The Stock Solution: p. 24UR; ©Dennis Cox/ChinaStock:
pp. 25UR, 26UR, 27LR; ©Christopher Liu/ChinaStock: pp. 25L, 26CR, 27UL, 28L, 30UR, 30LL; ChinaStock: p. 26UL; James Cloutier: pp. 29L,
30LR; ©Elaine Faris Keenan: pp. 34UL, 34LL, 36UL, 37UR, 37LL, 38UR, 38LR, 40UL, 40LL, 40LR; David Stoecklein/The Stock Solution: pp. 34UR,
35UR, 38UL, 39UR; Don Marshall/The Stock Solution: p. 35LL; CORBIS/Michael S. Yamashita: p. 36UR; CORBIS/Craig Lovell: p. 39LL.
All project photos by James Cloutier.
[**Photo credit key:** First Letter: U-Upper; C-Center, L-Lower; Second letter: R-Right; L-Left]

Library of Congress Cataloging-in-Publication Data
Tull, Mary.
    Northern Asia / Mary Tull, Tristan Franklin, and Cynthia A. Black.
        p.   cm. — (Artisans around the world)
    Includes bibliographical references and index.
    Summary: Describes the cultures of Mongolia, South Korea, China, and Japan and gives instructions for projects that
introduce local crafts of each country.
    ISBN 0-7398-0119-8
    1. Handicraft — China — Juvenile literature. 2. Handicraft — Mongolia—Juvenile literature. 3. Handicraft — Korea
(South) — Juvenile literature. 4. Handicraft — Japan — Juvenile literature. 5. China — Social life and customs —
Juvenile literature. 6. Mongolia — Social life and customs — Juvenile literature. 7. Korea (South) — Social life and
customs — Juvenile literature. 8. Japan — Social life and customs — Juvenile literature. [1. Handicraft — China.
2. Handicraft — Mongolia. 3. Handicraft — Korea (South). 4. Handicraft — Japan. 5. China — Social life and customs.
6. Mongolia — Social life and customs. 7. Korea (South) — Social life and customs. 8. Japan — Social life and customs.]
I. Franklin, Tristan. II. Black, Cynthia A. III. Title. IV. Series.
TT101.T85   1999
745.5'095 — dc21   98-49462
                                                                                                        CIP   AC

Printed and bound in the United States
1 2 3 4 5 6 7 8 9 0 WO 03 02 01 00 99

Table of Contents

The icons next to the projects in the Table of Contents identify the easiest and the most challenging project in the book. This may help you decide which project to do first.

⇨ easiest project

✪ most challenging project

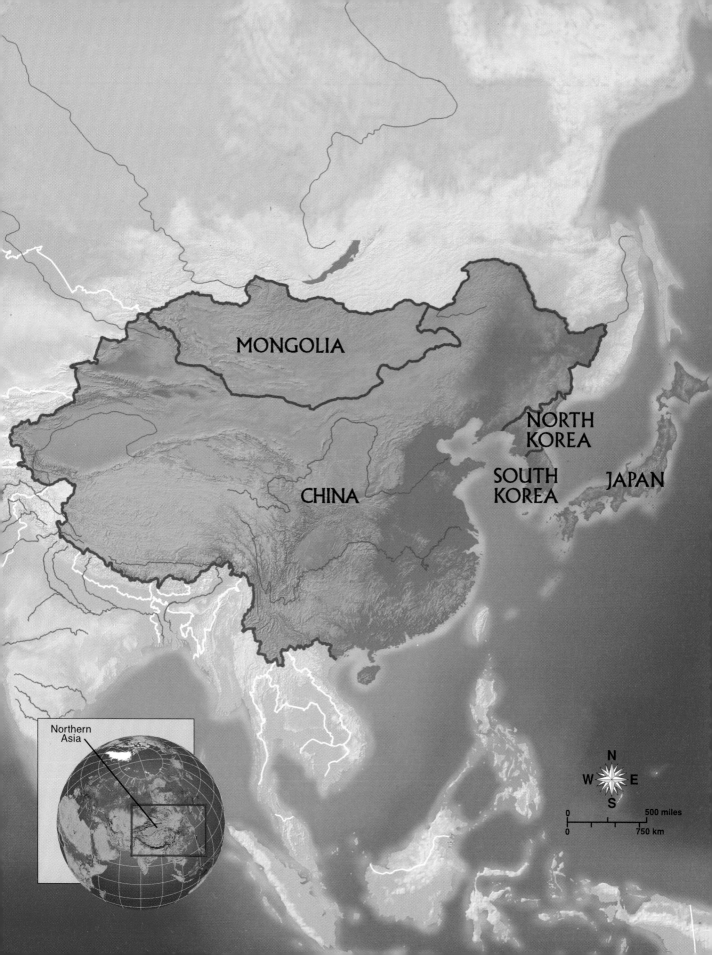

MONGOLIA

NORTH
KOREA

SOUTH
KOREA

JAPAN

CHINA

Northern
Asia

N
W   E
S

0 _____ 500 miles
0 _____ 750 km

Introduction to Artisans Around the World

There are many ways to learn about the history and present-day life of people in other countries. In school, students often study the history of a country to learn about its people. In this series, you will learn about the history, geography, and the way of life of groups of people through their folk art. People who create folk art are called **artisans.** They are skilled in an art, a craft, or a trade. You will then have a chance to create your own folk art, using your own ideas and symbols.

What Is Folk Art?

Folk art is not considered "fine art." Unlike many fine artists, folk artisans do not generally go to school to learn how to do their art. Very few folk artists are known as "famous" outside of their countries or even their towns. Folk art is the art of everyday people of a region. In this series, folk art also includes primitive art, that is, the art of the first people to be in an area. But, beware! Do not let this fool you into thinking that folk art is not "real" art. As you will see, the quality of the folk art in this series is amazing by any standards.

Folk art comes from the heart and soul of common people. It is an expression of their feelings. Often, it shows their personal, political, or religious beliefs. It may also have a practical purpose or meet a specific need, such as the need for shelter. In many cases, the folk art in the "Artisans Around the World" series comes from groups of people who did not even have a word for art in their culture. Art was simply what people did. It was a part of being human.

Introduction to *Northern Asia*

In this book, you will learn about these crafts and the people who do them:

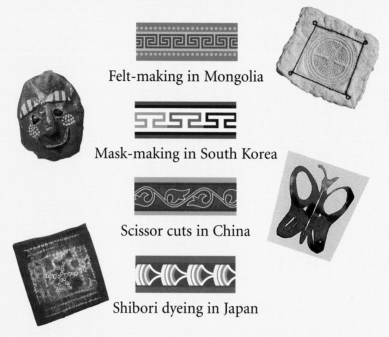

Felt-making in Mongolia

Mask-making in South Korea

Scissor cuts in China

Shibori dyeing in Japan

Then you will learn how to do projects of your own.

Here are some questions to think about as you read this book:

Which folk arts were ways to solve practical problems?
Which folk arts met specific needs?

Which folk arts expressed people's religious, political, or personal views?

Were some of these folk arts traditionally created mostly by men or by women?
Why do you think that was so? Is it still true today?

How did the history of a country influence some folk art traditions?

How did the geography, including the natural resources, of a country
influence some folk art traditions? How did people get folk art materials
that they needed but that were not found in their region?

Do some folk art traditions tell a story about a group of people or a culture?
If so, in what way?

How have these folk art traditions been passed down from generation to generation?

Folk Art Today

Reading about these folk art traditions, as well as creating your own folk art,
will increase your respect for the people who first did them.
Do you think some of these art forms, such as scissor cuts,
could be created faster or more easily using machines,
like electric scissors, or technology, like the computer?
Do you think anything would be lost by doing so, even if it were possible?

All of these folk art traditions of Northern Asia began long ago.
Can you think of any new folk art traditions being started now, in the
United States or in other countries? If so, what are they?
If not, why do you think there are no new traditions?

Safety Guidelines

These folk art projects are a lot of fun to do, but it's important to follow basic safety rules as you work. Here are some guidelines to help as you complete the projects in this book. Work slowly and carefully. That way you can enjoy the process.

1. Part of being a responsible person of any age is knowing when to ask for help. Some of these projects are challenging. Ask an adult for help whenever you need it. Even where the book does not tell you to, feel free to ask for help if you need it.

2. When painting, protect your clothing with an old shirt or a smock. When wet, acrylic paint can be removed with water. After it dries, it cannot be removed.

3. Handle all pointed tools, such as scissors, in a safe manner. Keep them stored in a safe place when not in use.

4. Dye Safety
   • Make sure an adult is present when you are dyeing.
   • Dyes will stain clothes, tables, floors, and skin. Cover every surface with plastic. Wear an apron to protect your clothes. Wear rubber gloves to protect your hands.
   • Dye powders can be harmful if inhaled. Wear a dust mask until the powder is dissolved in water.
   • Do not use the dye pot or mixing containers for food. Thoroughly wash dye out of the sink.

By the way, part of being an artist involves cleaning up! Be sure to clean up your work area when you are finished. Also, remember to thank anyone who helped you.

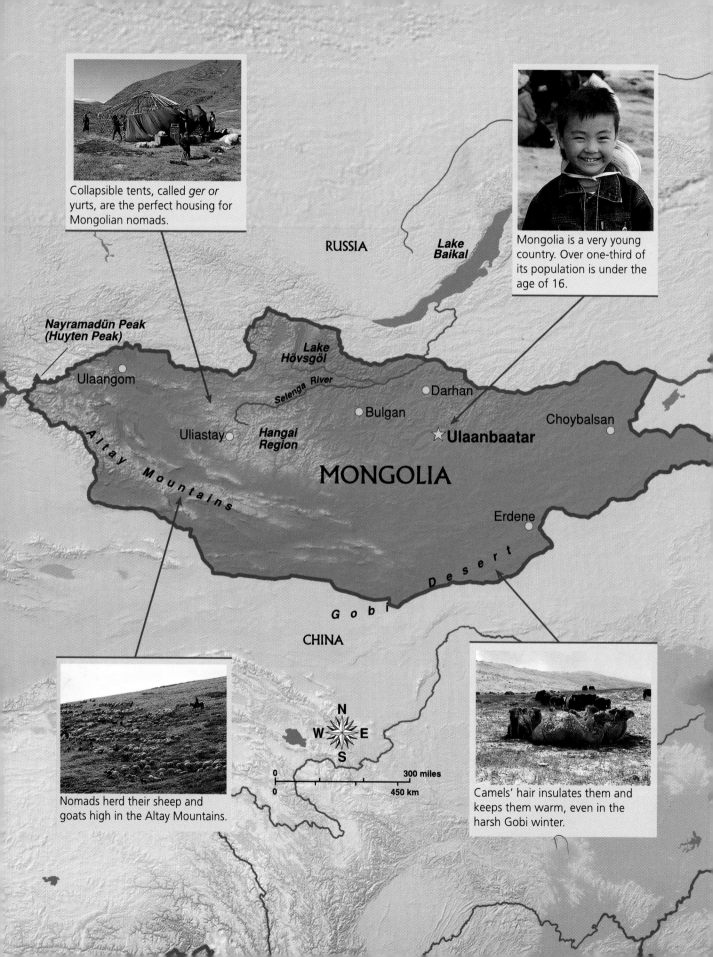

Collapsible tents, called *ger or yurts*, are the perfect housing for Mongolian nomads.

Mongolia is a very young country. Over one-third of its population is under the age of 16.

RUSSIA

Lake Baikal

Nayramadün Peak (Huyten Peak)

Ulaangom

Lake Hövsgöl

Selenga River

Darhan

Bulgan

Choybalsan

Uliastay

Hangai Region

★**Ulaanbaatar**

Altay Mountains

MONGOLIA

Erdene

Gobi Desert

CHINA

N
W E
S

0   300 miles
0   450 km

Nomads herd their sheep and goats high in the Altay Mountains.

Camels' hair insulates them and keeps them warm, even in the harsh Gobi winter.

Mongolia

▲ Ulaanbaatar's tall buildings and factories contrast sharply with the desert, plains, and rugged mountains that make up much of Mongolia.

Mongolia Facts

Name: Mongolia, "Land of the Blue Sky"
Capital: Ulaanbaatar
Borders: China, Russia
Population: 2.3 million
Language: Official language: Mongolian; Russian and English also spoken
Size: 604,250 sq. mi. (1,565,000 sq km); Mongolia is the largest land-locked country in the world
High/Low Points: Huyten Peak 14,350 ft. (4,374 m); no point in Mongolia lies less than 1,700 ft. (518 m) above sea level
Climate: Temperatures vary from a very hot 102° F (39° C) to a very cold -50° F (-46° C); little rain; occasional violent earthquakes
Wildlife: 426 species of birds; wild horses; camels; snow leopards; gazelles; the rare argali, or wild sheep; Gobi bear; ibex; donkeys
Plants: Siberian larch, cedar, pine, birch

A Study in Contrasts

Long ago, the mighty ruler Genghis Khan (also spelled Chingis Khan) rode across the Mongolian windswept plains. He would hardly recognize the Mongolia of today – an Asian country of over 2.3 million people. Over 600,000 people live in Ulaanbaatar (Ulan Bator), Mongolia's capital. This modern city has hotels, high-rise buildings, and an opera house. Mongolians look forward to the future, but they also feel a deep pride in their country's history and traditions.

"The Land of Felt"

The Mongolia of Genghis Khan's time can be most easily imagined in the sparsely populated, grass-covered plateaus, called the **steppes.** For centuries, nomads traveled these vast, rolling plains. These herders wandered in constant search of grazing land and water for their livestock.

Sheep are the most valuable livestock in Mongolia. They provide the nomads with food, material for tents and clothing, and manure for fuel. Sheep also supply the wool used to make felt.

Felt is the perfect material for a nomadic life. It can be made in a short time using very little equipment. It can also be made in different thicknesses. Heavy felt is used to make thick, wind-proof tents. A lighter felt is used for clothing. In the 4th century B.C., the Chinese called the steppes "the land of felt."

◀ This Mongolian family gathers for a meal in their yurt.

◄ A yurt and the herd of animals are very important to a nomadic way of life. Cheese is kept safe from animals by storing it in a bag on top of the yurt.

Nomadic Life

Nomads live in *gers,* or **yurts.** These tentlike homes are covered with felt. Yurts offer protection against the harsh winds and cold winter nights. They are easy to put up, take down, and move. Before there were roads, nomads used horses or camels to carry their yurts and other supplies across the steppes. Today, some nomads use jeeps and motorcycles to haul their gear and supplies.

Mongolia's Geography

Mongolia has four main geographic zones. The harsh Gobi Desert runs through southern Mongolia and into China. This windswept, treeless desert covers over 500,000 square miles (1,300,000 sq km). It is a treasure chest of fossilized dinosaur bones and eggs. To the east, the steppes extend hundreds of miles to Mongolia's eastern border. Mongolia has two mountainous regions. The Hangai is a forested region in the north central part of the country. The Altay Mountains in western Mongolia extend for hundreds of miles from Siberia to the Gobi. This treeless region contains Mongolia's highest peak and the only glaciers left in Mongolia.

Each geographic zone is different, but all zones share the bitter Mongolian climate. Each area also contains large areas of pasture that support thousands of herders.

Mongolian Horses

The steppes are the home of Mongolian horses, which are smaller and shaggier than other breeds. Their tough, stocky bodies help them to withstand a climate with extreme temperatures and little vegetation.

"Land of the Blue Sky"

Long ago, the Mongols called their region the "Land of the Blue Sky." It was for good reason. Mongolia averages 250 days of sunshine a year. The crystal-clear night sky is filled with stars that seem to touch the horizon.

The Gobi is a nearly ▶ treeless, windswept desert that stretches for more than 500,000 sq. mi. (1,300,000 sq km) across part of southern Mongolia and northern China.

The Mighty Genghis Khan

More than seven hundred years ago, nomadic tribes roamed Mongolia's vast grasslands and mountain ranges. They tamed horses and raised livestock. They were excellent archers and horsemen. Genghis Khan's military genius united these tribes into a unified, disciplined fighting force. Khan's army had strong bows and plenty of horses. They even carried collapsible bridges for surprise water crossings! The Mongol Empire was one of the strongest empires in Asian history.

▲ Today, Mongolians in the high mountains must help each other and work together to survive. These men are riding off to cut hay.

Mongolia Today

Mongolia is now a democratic country. An astonishing 85 percent of the population vote in elections. Their constitution, adopted in 1992, has been praised as one of the best ever written.

Mongolia's shift to a democratic, open form of government has been challenging, and there are many problems to solve. One of Mongolia's most urgent problems is overpopulation. Although it is a vast country, Mongolia's rapidly growing population is taxing the ability of the land to feed and support its people. Mongolians have a deep respect for their land and natural resources. They search for solutions to economic and social problems. But Mongolians weigh the economic benefits of oil, coal, and mining operations against the impact of such decisions on the environment.

Genghis Khan

Mongol conqueror Genghis Khan founded one of the largest land empires in history. He also promoted **literacy** – the ability to read and write – among his people. Today, Mongolia's literacy rate is between 80 and 90 percent.

Sending Messages

Genghis Khan developed the *yam*, a network of riders, to send messages over long distances. Riders bandaged and oiled their bodies to protect themselves against the harsh weather. They rode day and night, stopping only to change horses. By changing horses often, a good rider could cover as many as 200 miles in one day.

Genghis Khan's men often rode horses standing up, which worked to their advantage. Many people thought they were being invaded by giants!

TIMELINE

about 1162
Genghis Khan is born.

1691
Outer Mongolia comes under Manchu rule and remains a Chinese province until 1911.

1921
Mongolian People's Party established.

1961
Mongolia admitted to the United Nations.

1992
Mongolia's constitution is adopted on January 13th.

1280
Greatest extent of the Mongol Empire.

1911
Mongolians proclaim their independence.

1924
Mongolian People's Republic becomes the second Communist country in the world.

1990
Pro-democracy protests held in Ulaanbaatar.

1996
Mongolian Democratic Coalition defeats Communist Party in election.

▲ This group of women work together to beat the wool that will be made into felt. Children learn the art of felt-making from their parents and older people.

Making Felt

Large pieces of felt are often made outdoors in the late summer. Men and women work together to make these large pieces. The process begins by blessing the wool fleece. Then, it is beaten with sticks to separate the fibers and remove dirt.

A blanket-sized piece of old felt, the *mother felt,* is rolled out onto the field. It will be used to press and bind the new felt together. Three layers of new wool are stacked on it. One way is to place the best and whitest wool on the bottom. It will become the right side of the felt. Unwashed whole fleeces are put down next. Coarse brown wool is placed on top.

Warm water is splashed over the wool to wet it. Then, the mother felt and new wool are rolled tightly around a long pole. Wet hides are wrapped around the roll with strong rope. The bundle is tied to a camel, or to two horses. It is pulled over the steppes for several hours to pack it down. After the felt is made, it's time for a celebration!

▲ The stitched patterns help hold the felt together, making it stronger and more durable.

Quilted Felt

Different types of feltwork are created in various regions by different groups of Mongolian nomads. The Torgut people live around Bulgan, a remote region in northwest Mongolia in the Altay Mountains. Torgut women are known for their densely quilted patterns. They work together to stitch intricate patterns into the wool's natural off-white color. Some groups use undyed camel hair, spun on a spindle, for thread. The Torgut people use black yarn made of goat hair so the design will stand out.

Felt Quilting Patterns

Geometric or other design shapes are stitched into the felt. Images of people or animals are not used. The designs often have a special meaning. For example, the "endless knot" pattern means long life and prosperity. Traditional designs include:

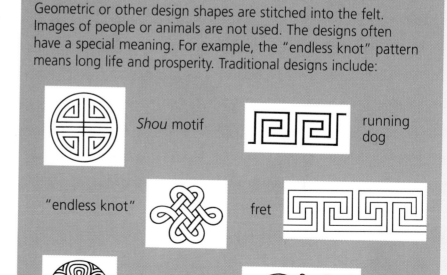

Shou motif

running dog

"endless knot"

fret

flower

spiral

Tools

- pair of wool carders
- square plastic washtub
- spray bottle
- wire brush
- heavy PVC pipe, 2 in. (5 cm) wide by 1 ft. (30 cm) or longer. A rolling pin will also work.
- iron-on transfer pencil or a non-permanent fabric marking pen
- embroidery needle
- pins

Materials

- 1 oz. (31 g) clean wool fleece from a craft store or a sheep farm
- laundry soap flakes (not detergent)
- hot water
- small piece of plastic wrap
- 1 yd. (1 m) cotton fabric
- heavy-duty rubber bands
- large plastic garbage bag
- pencil and paper
- heavy carpet thread
- thick yarn

Hot water, soap, and rubbing are all it takes to turn fleece into felt. ▼

You will experience the entire felt-making process, starting with the raw fleece and ending with decorated felt.

Prepare the Fleece

Different breeds of sheep have different kinds of fleece. When you are shopping for fleece, look for fibers that are fine and fluffy. Coarse, wiry fibers won't work as well. Also, look for short fibers about one inch (2.5 cm) long.

1. Begin by *carding* the fleece, or combing all the fibers in the same direction. Put a small handful of fleece on one carder. Hold the carder on your knee with the handle pointing away from you. Pull the other carder gently across the top toward you several times. Don't let the teeth of the two carders hook together. (You can also buy pre-carded fleece.) *(See diagram.)*

2. Remove the strip of carded fleece from the carders. Lay it in the bottom of the plastic tub. Card more fleece, covering the bottom of the tub with an even layer of strips. Line up the strips of fleece in rows facing the same direction. Overlap the edges like roof tiles. *(See diagram.)*

3. Card three or four more layers of fleece. Line up each new layer across the last. The completed stack of fleece should be about four or five inches (10-12 cm) thick. *(See diagram.)*

4. Check for thin spots by gently pressing the stack down with your hand. Patch any thin spots with bits of carded fleece.

Prepare the Fleece

1. Card the fleece.

2. First layer of strips.

3. Add 3-4 more layers.

layer 4

layer 3

layer 2

layer 1

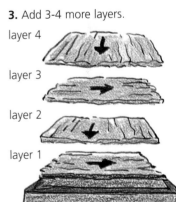

Experiment with Felt-making

Felt-making seems like magic, but it really makes perfect sense. Wool fibers have little scales on them. When you pour hot water on the fibers, they swell and the scales open up. The soap makes the fibers slippery so that they slide around and get tangled. As you rub the wool, the fibers compress and the scales hook together.

1. Dissolve 1 tablespoon (2 g) of soap flakes in one cup (1/4 liter) of hot water. Pour this solution into a spray bottle. Spray the fleece with a little of the soap solution. Sprinkle it with water that is as hot as your hands can stand.

2. Gently press the fleece with your fingertips. Rub in little circles, always going in the same direction. Work around the edges first, and then move toward the center. Rub slowly and gently so the layers don't shift or bunch up. *(See diagram.)*

3. After five minutes, flip the fleece over. The bottom side should be partially matted already. Drain the water from the tub and add more hot water. Add more soap if necessary. The soap suds should ooze up between your fingers a little. Too much soap, however, will make the fleece too slippery, and it won't mat together.

4. Continue to work on the felt, first on one side and then on the other. Add hot water and soap as needed. Check the condition of your felt every five minutes. It's easier to fix problems early in the process. See Helpful Hints for solutions to some problems.

5. After 20 to 30 minutes, your felt should be evenly matted and ready for *fulling*. This rolling process firms and shrinks the felt. Several pieces of felt can be fulled together at the same time.

6. Spread out a piece of cotton fabric. Arrange the pieces of felt on top so that they aren't touching each other.

7. Roll the felt and the fabric tightly around a thick plastic pipe or rolling pin. (If you use a good rolling pin, rinse the soap out of the felt first.) Fasten the bundle with several heavy rubber bands. *(See diagram.)*

◀ This rolling process, called *fulling*, will firm and shrink the felt.

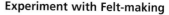

Experiment with Felt-making
2. Rub the fleece in little circles.

Helpful Hints

■ Trim off any loose tufts of wool. Rough up the edges around any clipped spots with a wire brush. Then spray with soap and work on the area some more.

■ To patch thin spots, first rough up the edges with a wire brush. Lay a piece of new fleece on top. Spray with soap and rub until it attaches.

■ If the fleece begins to hurt your fingers, rub it through a piece of plastic wrap. This also helps to keep the fleece from sticking to your fingers.

7. Roll the felt and fabric around a pipe.

Stitches You Will Use

Thread a needle and tie a knot at the end of the thread. You may use a single or double thread. Start sewing from the back of the felt so the knot will be hidden.

running stitch – Sew in and out of the fabric in a straight line. Make stitches that are even in length.

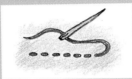

couching stitch – Sew over the top of the yarn, with a tiny stitch every 1/2-inch (1 cm) or so.

8. Place the bundle on the ground on a plastic garbage bag. Sprinkle it with more hot water. Roll the bundle of felt back and forth vigorously with your hands or feet. Open the roll every five minutes. Turn the felt pieces 90 degrees, or flip them front to back. Continue fulling until the felt is firm and strong.

9. You can stop at any stage and finish up later. Rinse the soap solution out completely, though, because it will weaken the wool. Add a teaspoon (5 ml) of vinegar to neutralize the soap. Spread the felt out to dry flat on a towel. Press it with a steam iron set on medium heat ("wool" setting).

Quilt the Felt

1. Make a pattern.

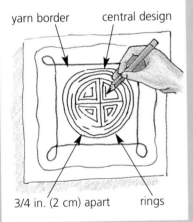

yarn border · central design

3/4 in. (2 cm) apart · rings

Quilt the Felt

To get ideas for your quilting pattern, study the Mongolian designs on page 12. In traditional patterns, the central design is often repeated in larger and larger rings. Sometimes a border of thick yarn is applied.

1. Make a pattern for your design. Trace around the felt on paper. Draw a thick line where you want the yarn border. Then draw your design in the central space. Repeat the design as shown. Space the rings about 3/4-inch (2 cm) apart. *(See diagram.)*

2. Transfer the pattern. Because felt is so soft, carbon paper won't work. Instead, trace over your pattern with an iron-on transfer pencil. Place the pattern face down on the felt, and iron to transfer. Or, draw your design freehand using a non-permanent fabric marking pen.

3. For quilting, use heavy carpet thread in a color that contrasts with your felt. Sew along the lines of the design, using a *running stitch*. Push the needle straight up and down. Pull the thread tightly so that it sinks into the felt.

4. Lay a piece of heavy yarn along the line of the border. Pin it in several places. Thread a needle with sewing thread that matches the yarn. Use a *couching stitch* to attach the yarn to the felt.

These handmade ▶ felt pieces, quilted by students, are wonderful to touch and to see.

Korean religious and cultural festivals often include dance. Each dance has its own style of movement to add meaning to the event.

CHINA

RUSSIA

Tumen River

Mount Paektu

Ch'ongjin

Yalu River

NORTH KOREA

Sinuiju

Korea Bay

★ **P'yongyang**

Koreans enjoy many different types of games. *Ch'ajon Nori*, is played for fun and to promote team spirit.

SEA OF JAPAN

★ **Seoul**

YELLOW SEA

SOUTH KOREA

Today, Seoul's ancient Toksugung Palace is surrounded by modern office buildings.

Taejon

Naktong River

Taegu

Pusan

Brush-painting, a Korean form of calligraphy, was developed about 1,500 years ago.

Korea Strait

JAPAN

N
W E
S

0   100 miles
0   150 km

Cheju Island

Mount Halla

South Korea

Korea Facts

Name: South Korea
(Republic of Korea)
Capital: Seoul
Population: 45,948,811
Size: 38,025 sq. mi.
(98,484 sq km)
High/Low Points: Hallasan
(Mount Halla), 6,398 ft. (1,950 m);
sea level

Name: North Korea (Democratic
People's Republic of Korea)
Capital: P'yongyang
Population: 24,317,004
Size: 46,450 sq. mi.
(120,538 sq km)
High/Low Points: Mount Paektu
(Mountain of Eternal Snow)
9,003 ft. (2,744 m); sea level

Korean peninsula:
Language: Korean
(about six dialects)
Water: Yellow Sea, Sea of Japan,
Korea Strait; Yalu, Tumen,
Naktong rivers
Borders: China and Russia
Climate: Dry, cold winters;
hot, humid, rainy summers;
temperatures range from about
87° F (31° C) in Aug. to 32° F
(0° C) in Feb.; monsoons affect
Korea's weather
Plants: 4,500 native varieties of
plants; the largest and oldest fruit-
bearing tree in the world is the
Great Gingko tree, planted in the
10th century on the temple
grounds of Yongmunsa Temple
Wildlife: Boars, bears, deer,
wildcats, wolves, hares, weasels,
badgers, Korean tigers, leopards

Seoul, a Modern City

Seoul, South Korea's capital, looks like many modern cities. It is both an ancient city and a fast-paced urban center. It is also one of the largest cities in the world.

Seoul was established as Korea's capital before Columbus traveled to America. It became the capital of South Korea when the Republic of Korea was formed in 1948. Seoul holds more than 600 years of Korean culture and tradition. Its modern skyscrapers and traffic jams make it hard to imagine the time when it was the center of the "Hermit Kingdom." This name was given to Korea because in the 1600s Korea's rulers closed the country to all foreigners for almost 200 years.

▲ Myongdong, Seoul's center of finance and fashion, offers shoppers cultural and sports activities, as well as many things to buy.

Ties to Ancient Traditions

Walking through Seoul's neighborhoods, visitors can see the Korean people's ties to ancient traditions. Most families in the South honor their ancestors in special ceremonies. Children still show respect by bowing to their grandparents.

Beautiful temples are a symbol of Korea's ancient religious traditions. Palaces recall its history of strong rulers and powerful **dynasties,** or ruling families. Ancient traditions are also seen today in Korea's artists, dancers, and actors. These artists, including the mask dancers, perform for the South Korean people and for tourists.

◀ When a Korean girl turns fourteen, she wears beautiful traditional clothing in a special ceremony to celebrate her coming of age.

▲ The guarded and fenced Demilitarized Zone separates North and South Korea.

In the Shadow of Powerful Neighbors

Korea's geographic location has greatly affected its history. It is a mountainous **peninsula** surrounded on three sides by water. Three powerful countries – China, Japan, and Russia – are its neighbors. Throughout its history, Korea has been invaded and controlled for long periods of time by these and other countries. The United States Army fought there during the Korean War in the 1950s. The fight for Korea by foreign powers has resulted in two Koreas, South Korea and North Korea.

South Korea and North Korea are separated from each other by a high fence and two very different forms of government. South Korea is a representative democracy. North Korea is a Communist country that shares a border with China and Russia.

"The Land of the Morning Calm"

South Koreans refer to their country as "The Land of the Morning Calm." The name recalls a peaceful time. In spite of its stormy history, its people have survived. Although they have borrowed elements from Chinese and Japanese culture, they also have kept their own cultural identity. Many art forms, including the mask dance dramas, are distinctly Korean, even though they are performed in other Asian countries.

The Flag of the Republic of Korea

The South Korean flag is unlike most flags of the world. It does not contain symbols of politics, geography, or historic events. Instead, its symbols come from Asian philosophy. These yin and yang symbols stand for balance between elements like good and evil, night and day, fire and water, and the masculine and feminine. The bars in each corner stand for heaven (unbroken lines) and earth (broken lines).

During the Japanese occupation (1910-1945), the Korean flag was taken down and hidden. On Liberation Day the flags were flown again as a symbol of Korea's struggle for freedom.

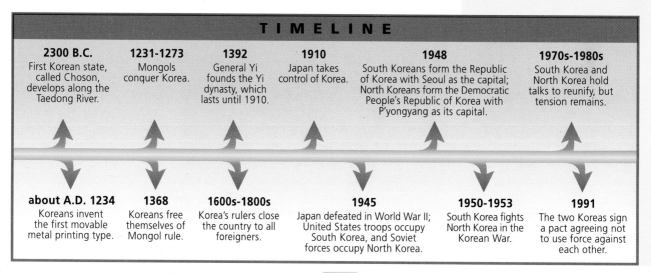

TIMELINE

2300 B.C.
First Korean state, called Choson, develops along the Taedong River.

1231-1273
Mongols conquer Korea.

1392
General Yi founds the Yi dynasty, which lasts until 1910.

1910
Japan takes control of Korea.

1948
South Koreans form the Republic of Korea with Seoul as the capital; North Koreans form the Democratic People's Republic of Korea with P'yongyang as its capital.

1970s-1980s
South Korea and North Korea hold talks to reunify, but tension remains.

about A.D. 1234
Koreans invent the first movable metal printing type.

1368
Koreans free themselves of Mongol rule.

1600s-1800s
Korea's rulers close the country to all foreigners.

1945
Japan defeated in World War II; United States troops occupy South Korea, and Soviet forces occupy North Korea.

1950-1953
South Korea fights North Korea in the Korean War.

1991
The two Koreas sign a pact agreeing not to use force against each other.

Mask Dance Dramas

There are three major categories of Korean mask dance dramas with ten different styles:

Sandae – dance dramas originating in the courts of rulers of the Choson Period (1392-1910) or of earlier periods

Sonangje – dance dramas performed at village religious festivals, in which the dancers make fun of the powerful people in society

Sajagye – the lion mask play that came from China in the Silla Period (57 B.C.–A.D. 935). It is now performed in Bukchong County in North Korea. One drama that includes the Lion Dance is the *Pyolshin Guttal Nori* of Hahoe Village. It originally used 14 masks. Now, 11 masks are used. These masks are now national treasures.

The Mask Dance Drama

The mask dances of Korea come from traditions that are hundreds of years old. This art form is more than just dances performed by dancers wearing masks. Each dance tells a story. The dancers act out the parts of people, animals, or supernatural beings.

Centuries ago, the mask dance dramas were performed at court for the ruling class. They were often Buddhist dramas that taught lessons about how to behave and live. Later, during the Choson Period (1392-1910), the mask dance

▲ This fearsome-looking character is important in Korean folklore. He is one of the four guardian kings of the cardinal directions—East, West, North, and South.

dramas came under the control of common people. The stories, masks, and dance movements became a series of short plays that allowed common people to express their anger at the nobility and at religious leaders. In the original version of one play, a lion devoured those who did not follow Buddhist principles. During the Choson period the lion instead devoured a corrupt priest.

Mask Dances Today

Today in Seoul visitors can see the Bongsan Masked Dance or the *Yangju Pyol Sandae Nori*. The Bongsan dancing style is very demanding, with lots of leaps, squats, and big movements. The masks are made to look very **grotesque,** or ugly, in order to be funny. The *Yangju* dance style is more elegant and smooth. *Yangju* masks are more realistic in design.

Audience Participation

The audience plays an important part in the drama of any dance performance. By the end it is not unusual for people in the audience to join in the dance. This is especially true in rural areas. In the country, the dancers often perform on hillsides. After the performance ends, both the performers and audience parade down into the town.

◄ *Ch'oyongmu* is one of the oldest Korean mask dances.

The Design of the Dance Masks

Korean artisans have always made masks from materials at hand, such as wood, paper, gourds, and fur. It is easy to see why dancers prefer the light weight of paper and gourd masks! The dance masks are designed to cover only the face. The dancers wear black cloths to cover the back and sides of their head and neck.

The colors of the masks are chosen for their traditional meaning and their ability to be seen. Red, black, and white are used often. An old person's mask is black, which also stands for the north. A young man's mask is red, which is a symbol of the south and summer. White is used for a young woman's mask. Traditionally, bright colors and **exaggerated** facial features helped the masks to be seen when the dramas were performed around wood fires at night.

Creating a Character in a Mask

Masks represent, or stand for, many different characters. There are masks for human faces as well as for animals and gods. Masks may represent real people as well as imaginary beings. Sometimes the expressions and shapes are exaggerated and odd-looking. Other facial masks may show contempt or anger. The masks of wealthy, aristocratic men are almost always distorted, or exaggerated, in order to make fun of them. They have strange eyes, lopsided noses, and uneven lips.

▲ This mask dance, like many others from the folk tradition, makes fun of certain types of people in Korean society.

◀ *Ogwangdae-nori* mask dances use costumes, crowns, and facial expressions to make fun of the ruling class.

Tools

- pencil
- scissors
- paintbrushes
- awl, or pointed tool
- needle with large eye

Materials

- paper
- newspapers
- masking tape
- pieces of thick cardboard
- smooth cord, or thin rope
- papier-mâché paste
- white latex enamel paint
- acrylic paints
- polyurethane sealer
- bits of fake fur or wool fleece (optional)
- white craft glue
- elastic, 3/4-in. (2 cm) wide
- 1/2 yd. (45 cm) black or white cloth
- carpet thread
- yarn

Work with friends to make several different mask characters. Then put on your own mask drama!

Plan Your Mask

1. Work with several friends to decide on the characters for your mask drama. Korean dance masks depict common types of people in Korean society. What are common types of people in our own society? They might include a hero, a villain, a grandparent, or a student. Think of characters who will interact together in an interesting way.

2. Draw a plan of the mask you will create. It should show a general type of character, not an individual. It's not supposed to look real. Study Korean masks for ideas. Use each part of the face to help show the type of person you're creating. Will the face look evil, silly, or wise? What expression is typical of your character's personality?

Make the Mask Framework

1. Open and stack together four full sheets of newspaper. Roll the longer side into a tight tube and tape in several places. Make another tube in the same way. Overlap the ends of the two tubes to make one long tube. Tape securely.

2. Shape the long tube into an oval frame that fits around your face. The top of the frame should sit on the front of your head. The bottom should reach a few inches under your chin. Overlap and tape the ends of the tube. Mold the frame into a shape you like. *(See diagram.)*

3. Open and stack together five more full sheets of newspapers. Draw an oval the same shape as your frame, but three inches (8 cm) bigger all around. Cut out this large oval through all five layers of newspaper. *(See diagram.)*

Make the Mask Framework

2. Shape the tube into a frame.

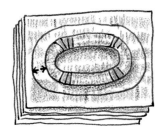

3. Draw an oval.

◄ Make the mask framework with rolled newspapers.

21

4. Cover the frame with the five-layer oval. Take tucks around the oval to make the mask puff out in front. Begin by taking a little tuck at the forehead. Tape the papers firmly to the top edge of the frame. Continue around, taking evenly spaced tucks. Use plenty of masking tape to strengthen the edges of the frame. *(See diagram.)*

5. Hold the mask up to your face. Feel for your eyes through the newspaper. Mark their location on the outside of the mask. Remove the mask, and cut eyeholes big enough to see through. Cut a mouth opening if you wish.

6. Form the larger features of the face. Cut big eyebrows from heavy cardboard. Roll a tube of newspaper for a long nose. Exaggerate the size and shape of all facial features. Tape them in place with lots of masking tape. *(See diagram.)*

7. Korean masks often have a raised outline around the eyes and lips. Thin eyebrows and skin wrinkles are also made with raised lines. To make raised lines, cut pieces of cord or thin rope. Tape them in place with small pieces of masking tape. *(See diagram.)*

8. Look at your mask framework from all angles. Make changes until the face looks right to you. Add masking tape to smooth the surfaces.

Papier-mâché the Mask

1. Cover your table with a plastic tablecloth or a garbage bag. Mix the papier-mâché paste and paper pulp. (See recipes under Helpful Hints.) Tear some newspapers into small strips.

2. Stuff wads of newspaper into a plastic bag. Place the bag under the mask framework for support as you papier-mâché. Use the paper pulp to form cheeks, lips, warts, or a chin for your mask.

3. Dip newspaper strips into the paste and apply them to the mask. Smooth the strips carefully around the cord outlines, so they won't be hidden. Cover all the features made with paper pulp to help hold them in place. Wrap strips around the edges of the frame and the edges of the eye and mouth openings.

4. Cover the entire face with four layers of newspaper strips. Use a generous amount of paste. If the surface begins to look pasty, however, apply some dry strips to soak up the excess. Make sure that all the tape is covered, and that the surface looks smooth.

5. Dry the mask for three days to one week.

Make the Mask Framework

4. Take tucks around the oval.

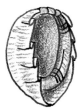

6. Form the larger features.

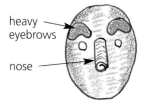

heavy eyebrows

nose

7. Cut cord for a raised line.

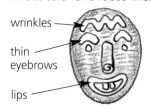

wrinkles

thin eyebrows

lips

Helpful Hints

■ **Papier-mâché paste:** Stir together 1/2 cup (75 g) flour and 2 tablespoons (28 g) salt with 1 cup (1/4 liter) warm water. Mix the paste with your fingers. It should feel like thick soup.

■ **Paper pulp:** Tear newspapers into tiny pieces. Get them wet with papier-mâché paste. Work and press the mixture a bit with your fingers until it becomes soft and moldable.

Finish the Mask

2-3. Paint your mask.

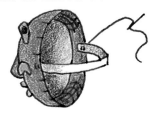

5. Sew the elastic to the frame.

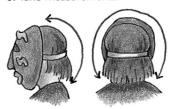

6. Take measurements.

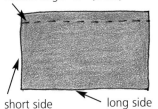

folded edge - 2" (5 cm)

short side   long side

7. Glue the cloth to the mask. Add a drawstring if you want.

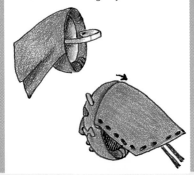

Finish the Mask

1. When the mask is dry and firm, spray or brush it with white enamel paint. Paint the inside as well, if you wish. The enamel will cover the newspaper ink. It will also help to make the mask stronger.

2. Mix acrylic paint for the base color of the mask. Choose a bold color, such as red, white, or black. **When painting, protect your clothing with an old shirt or a smock. When wet, acrylic paint can be removed with water. After it dries, it cannot be removed.** Paint the entire face with the base color, and let it dry. *(See diagram.)*

3. When the base color is dry, apply the other colors. Choose two colors that contrast with the base. Paint the lips and eyes. Paint stripes or spots on the eyebrows or cheeks. *(See diagram.)*

4. When all the paint is dry, seal it with polyurethane. Add fake fur or wool fleece for hair, eyebrows, or a beard if desired.

5. Hold the mask on your face. Cut a strong piece of elastic to stretch around your head, just above your ears. Make it tight enough to hold the mask in place, but not so tight that it's uncomfortable. Poke holes in the frame with an awl. Sew the elastic to each side of the frame with heavy thread. *(See diagram.)*

6. Make a cloth hood to cover your hair. While wearing your mask, take two measurements. For the short side, measure from the top of the mask to the back of your neck. Add two inches (5 cm) for the top folded edge. For the long side, measure from one shoulder and then around the edge of the mask frame to your other shoulder. *(See diagram.)*

7. Cut a piece of fabric using your measurements. Glue the long side of the cloth to the mask edge, draping it forward over the face. When the glue dries, fold the cloth back. If you want, sew a drawstring around the bottom edge of the hood to gather the fabric around your hair. *(See diagram.)*

8. Your mask is ready! Work with other students to write a play starring your mask characters. Act it out for your class or for family and friends.

Students' finished villain, ▶ clown, and grandmother masks.

Scientists believe that pandas lived on earth 600,000 years ago. Today pandas are listed as an endangered species.

This Chinese girl dances the Red Flag Dance.

The beautiful Pool of Nine Dragons east of Xi'an is a peaceful place to visit.

During the Lantern Festival people carry candlelit lanterns through the streets.

RUSSIA

Lake Baikal

Amur River

Songhua River

KAZAKHSTAN

MONGOLIA

Gobi Desert

Inner Mongolia

Beijing

NORTH KOREA

SEA OF JAPAN

SOUTH KOREA

KYRGYZSTAN

Turpan Depression

Taklimakan Desert

TAJIKISTAN

AFGHANISTAN

CHINA

PAKISTAN

Huang (Yellow) River

Shaanxi Province

Wei River

Xi'an

YELLOW SEA

Tibet

Mount Everest

Himalaya Range

NEPAL

BHUTAN

Chang (Yangtze) River

Wuhan

Shanghai

EAST CHINA SEA

INDIA

MYANMAR (BURMA)

LAOS

VIETNAM

Xi River

TAIWAN

Hong Kong

PACIFIC OCEAN

Hainan Island

N W E S

500 miles

750 km

China

China Facts

Name: China
(People's Republic of China)
Capital: Beijing
Borders: Russia, Mongolia, Kazakhstan, Kyrgyzstan, Tajikistan, Afghanistan, Pakistan, India, Nepal, Bhutan, Myanmar, Laos, Vietnam, North Korea
Population: 1.2 billion
Language: Official language: Mandarin
Size: 3,678,470 sq. mi. (9,527,200 sq km)
High/Low Points: Mount Everest, 29,028 ft. (8,848 m); Turpan Depression, 505 ft. (154 m) below sea level
Climate: Extremely wide temperature range from -22° F (-30° C) in January in the north to 82° F (28° C) in July in the south
Major Rivers: Chang (Yangtze), Huang (Yellow), Xi, Wei
Wildlife: Snow leopards, wild yaks, panda bears, moose, cranes, sables, herons
Plants: Bamboo, ginseng, the rare Cathay silver fir, angelica

Spring Festival in Shaanxi

It is Spring Festival time in Xi'an, the capital city of Shaanxi, a province in the east of central China. There is a hustle and bustle around town. People of all ages are excited about this special New Year celebration!

▲ Xi'an's Bell Tower is a huge building in the center of the city. A large iron bell rings the hours of the day.

Spring Festival is a special occasion for papercutting throughout China. Families make papercuts to decorate the inside and outside of their houses. In the days leading up to the festival, children watch while their mothers and grandmothers sit quietly and cut designs, often out of red paper. The rest of the family gives the house a thorough cleaning. They hope to sweep out any ill-will or bad fortune in order to make way for good luck in the new year.

The Festival Gets Underway

While families make papercuts to decorate their homes, artisans carve out pictures on thin, smooth-grained paper to sell at the festival. Children look on shyly as the artisans set up their tables and lay out their delicate, handmade tools. Soon the festival is underway. The streets are filled with merchants making and selling their papercuts.

◄ Many Chinese people believe that hanging a papercut made from red paper is a sign of good luck. During Spring Festival papercuts are placed on windows, walls, and ceilings to bring good fortune.

◄ Cai Lun, a man who worked for the emperor of China, invented a new method of papermaking. He made a mushy pulp out of fish nets, rags, and plants. He pressed the pulp into very thin sheets and allowed them to dry.

A Land of Ancient Beginnings

Evidence of early human life in China dates back perhaps 600,000 years. Shaanxi is one of the oldest settled regions in China. The first evidence of writing in the Shaanxi region appeared in 1200 B.C. However, it was not until much later that paper was used for writing.

The Beginnings of Paper and Papercuts

Paper was invented in A.D. 105. First, mulberry bark and later silk were used to make paper, perhaps because they were long lasting. The papermaking process was time-consuming and expensive. At first, paper was available only to the rich. It was another 800 years before all Chinese people could use paper.

The earliest known papercuts were discovered by archaeologists in 1959. They date from A.D. 514-551. It is believed that at first they were used for funeral and burial practices. Designs were cut out of paper and burned as gifts to escort the dead into another life.

Papermaking stayed a secret within China for a long time. It was not until A.D. 751 that the idea spread to the Middle East and then to Europe.

▲ Both single color and multicolor papercuts were seen as papercutting grew more popular. Some people made a living from their craft. They traveled from village to village selling their papercuts for patterns and as decorations for homes.

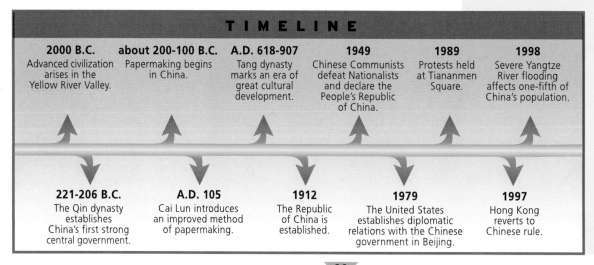

TIMELINE

2000 B.C.	about 200-100 B.C.	A.D. 618-907	1949	1989	1998
Advanced civilization arises in the Yellow River Valley.	Papermaking begins in China.	Tang dynasty marks an era of great cultural development.	Chinese Communists defeat Nationalists and declare the People's Republic of China.	Protests held at Tiananmen Square.	Severe Yangtze River flooding affects one-fifth of China's population.

221-206 B.C.	A.D. 105	1912	1979	1997
The Qin dynasty establishes China's first strong central government.	Cai Lun introduces an improved method of papermaking.	The Republic of China is established.	The United States establishes diplomatic relations with the Chinese government in Beijing.	Hong Kong reverts to Chinese rule.

Shaanxi, the Center of Art and Civilization in China

The Wei River cuts through the middle of Shaanxi. This rich, fertile belt became the center of Chinese civilization. By A.D. 618 the province contained the largest city in China. The booming city of Chang'an, now called Xi'an, was alive with merchants, entertainers, poets, and artists.

Today, Shaanxi province has a population of over 35 million. Most people live in the central and southern regions. The area has a mild climate and is lush and mountainous. Flower **templates,** or patterns, used for papercuts and other art forms, come from this region.

The Artisans of North Shaanxi

To the north, a dry plateau is covered by a thick blanket of loess, or loose soil deposited by the wind. This isolated area has steep cliffs and deep, narrow valleys, or **ravines.** The region's dry climate allows paper window decorations to be hung in windows and doorways.

The artisans of this region are mostly peasant women. Unlike people in the more populated regions, these artisans cut paper without using patterns. Because of the geographic isolation, influences of the outside world are slower to reach these villages. They do not have easy access to tools that are readily available in other areas. As a result, they have traditionally made their own. This has allowed the region to keep its unusual cutting styles.

Shaanxi is a region of mountains, where caves are dug out of the hills. During the cold Shaanxi winters, women sit on heated, built-in brick beds to do their papercuts or needlework.

The Army of Terra-cotta Warriors, one of China's most amazing historical sights, is located near Xi'an. In 1974, peasants digging a well uncovered an underground vault with thousands of life-size terra-cotta (clay) soldiers and their horses in battle formation. Although buried for more than 2,200 years, the soldiers' swords were still sharp.

Artistic Inspiration

When artists begin a new papercut, they need an idea. The ideas for papercuts may come from legends, spirit figures, daily life, or folktales. An artisan may create a papercut with specific symbols in honor of a special occasion or good luck wish. Designs found in the Shaanxi province show people leading their everyday lives. Such designs include an acrobat performing at a wedding, a mother feeding her child, and a man shearing his sheep.

If a pattern is used, it is drawn on a thick piece of paper. This way, it can be used many times. The artisan uses a brush and black ink to create the pattern design. Great care must be taken to connect all the parts of the pattern. Favorite patterns are often traded back and forth among friends.

"Pilgrims of the Rivers and Lakes"

Long ago, traveling artisans went from village to village, selling their papercuts. They were called "pilgrims of the rivers and lakes." Today, there are three levels of these papercutting artisans. The highest level of artisan is considered a professional. Part-time artists make up the second level of artisans. They may sell their papercuts at markets or cut paper on assembly lines. Amateurs make up the largest group of papercut artisans. Amateurs cut paper solely as a hobby. During festival time, all three groups of artisans can be seen making or selling their papercuts.

Chinese theater and opera often include acrobatics, martial arts, music, and dance. One traveling theater group, the Beijing Opera, is world famous.

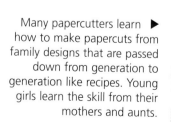

Many papercutters learn ▶ how to make papercuts from family designs that are passed down from generation to generation like recipes. Young girls learn the skill from their mothers and aunts.

Lotus – time (past, present, and future, because all the buds, flowers, and seedpods are all seen at the same time)

Loyalty of Duck and Drake – happy marriage

Tiger – courage

Xi – happiness

Papercutters use two different methods to make their cuts. Each method has its own purpose and technique, or method.

Scissor Cuts

In this method, the papercutter makes a continuous line in the paper, creating intricate illustrations. The scissors have large, oval handles and very short, sharp blades. Most of the cutting is done near the point where the scissor blades are connected. The tips are used only for trimming. It is a slow process, because only a few pieces can be cut at a time. This method is usually used by master artisans and by women, who create scissor cuts to decorate their houses.

Knife Cuts

Knives allow small details to be cut into the paper. Many papercuts are made at one time using this method. First, the bottom of a wooden box is covered with a mixture of charcoal and fat, which usually includes beeswax. Once this cutting surface hardens, it keeps the knives from being blunted. The surface is then dusted with flour, so that the paper can be easily removed later. Up to 50 sheets of tissue paper are laid in the box, topped with a pattern. The stack of papers is held in place with large stitches or nails. Great skill is needed to drive the tools straight down through the sheets of paper so the papers do not shift during cutting.

Many papercuts ▶ from northern China's agricultural areas feature farm animals such as oxen.

Papercut Colors

Many papercuts are black and white. However, the use of color adds drama, detail, and imagination to papercuts. Red is the preferred color, because it symbolizes joy, courage, and beauty. Papercutters use brightly colored dyes and watercolors to paint their papercuts. These colors are bolder than the paler shades used in traditional Chinese brush painting.

Styles of Papercuts

Chinese artisans often make their own special knives, punches, and chisels. Each tool is designed to cut a special shape in the paper. Because the kinds of tools vary, different styles and techniques are used. There are three basic styles of papercuts that can be seen during the Chinese New Year.

"Happy flowers" papercuts adorn the walls of houses for holidays such as Spring Festival. Families begin decorating many days before the holiday begins. By the time the day arrives, the house is full of these papercuts.

"Window flowers" are very delicate papercuts. In some villages, where glass is not available, families cover wooden window frames with white paper. They paste elaborate papercuts onto the white backgrounds. Whether on glass or on white paper, these cuts must be airy enough not to block the light coming into the house. Twenty years ago most windows in China were made of paper as they had been a thousand years earlier. Even palaces had paper windows!

"Hanging papers" or "hanging money" papercuts are usually hung in a row in doorways during New Year. Some believe that they welcome the God of Wealth.

▲ Detailed one-color papercuts are very dramatic. Sometimes different shades of a single color are used.

In the past, girls were taught papercutting in preparation for marriage. The groom's family judged a bride's intelligence by her skill in papercutting.

◀ The crane is a symbol of long life often used in papercut designs. Flower designs reflect the Chinese people's love of nature.

Tools

- pencil and eraser
- stapler
- scissors
- small embroidery scissors with short, pointed blades
- paintbrushes
- fine-point permanent black pen

Materials

- white typing paper
- white rice paper (Japanese mulberry paper); soft, thin drawing paper; or origami paper
- newspapers
- colored inks or watercolors
- heavy paper for mounting
- white glue and toothpick

Design a Scissor Cut

2. Draw inside spaces.
enclosed spaces

spaces with outlets

3. Shade in the solid parts.

bridge
island

Scissors are preferred for cutting paper at home in China. With scissors you can make surprisingly intricate and delicate papercuts.

Collect Ideas for Scissor Cuts

Before you make your own scissor cuts, look at many Chinese papercuts. Note the broad range of images. Gather and save your ideas.

Magazines are a good source of photos of people and things in nature. Look through family photographs. Examine your favorite book illustrations. Sketch trees, flowers, animals, and people around you. It is also okay to borrow an idea from another papercut! Copying is part of the papercutting tradition.

Design a Scissor Cut

Design a simple scissor cut to experiment with the process. Choose an easy image, such as a flower, butterfly, or bird.

1. Make a pattern on a quarter-sheet of white typing paper. Draw the outside outline of your image in the center of the paper. If you cut around this outline, you would have a very simple papercut, called a *silhouette*.

2. A silhouette has no spaces cut from the inside. It's the spaces that make a papercut look airy and delicate. Draw inside spaces on your pattern. Some spaces can have outlets to the outside. Others can be enclosed. *(See diagram.)*

3. Work with a pencil and eraser to improve your drawing. Gently shade in all the parts of the pattern that will be solid paper. The solid paper areas must be connected together in one flowing piece. Any part that is floating alone, like an island, will fall out when you cut. Connect an island to the rest of the design by drawing a bridge. *(See diagram.)*

Leave bridges so ▶ that when you cut, pieces won't fall out.

Experiment with Scissor Cuts

Think of your first few scissor cuts as experiments. See what you, the paper, and the scissors are capable of doing.

1. Choose the paper you will use. If you plan to paint your scissor cut, use white rice paper. It will absorb the paint or ink. Cut the paper the same size as your pattern. Put the pattern on top and staple the two pieces together around the edges. *(See diagram.)*

2. Now you're ready to cut. Read the hints at the right. Begin with the inside spaces. To start an enclosed space, hold the packet of paper on a thick stack of newspaper. Poke the point of your embroidery scissors into the center to make a small hole.

3. Next, cut the outside outline. Some kinds of curves are easier to cut than others. Feel free to change the design as you cut. It is this looseness that makes scissor cuts so appealing.

4. Make a few simple scissor cuts before you try something complex. Experiment with different kinds of paper. Try cutting several papers together. If your scissors are sharp, you can cut as many as six pieces at one time. Staple the layers together around the edges with the pattern on top.

Make a Scissor Cut Scene

Now, try a more complex design. How about a person doing something you enjoy? A favorite book illustration? An outdoor scene? Look through the images you collected for ideas.

1. Use a whole sheet of typing paper for the pattern. You can draw a built-in frame around the design if you wish. Make sure that all parts of the design are attached to the frame. *(See diagram.)*

2. Designing people in scissor cuts is a challenge. There are several ways to draw faces. Study the examples at the right. *(See diagram.)*

3. Revise and improve your design. Make sure that the solid parts are balanced with the spaces. The more paper you remove, the more delicate the scissor cut will be. These designs take time. Don't rush.

4. When you are completely satisfied, stack the papers and staple as before. Cut slowly and carefully.

Experiment with Scissor Cuts

1. Staple the pattern to the paper.

Helpful Hints

■ Use pointed embroidery scissors for tight inside spaces and little angles.

■ Use larger scissors for long, straight lines and gentle curves. Open the scissors wide and make slow, smooth cuts.

■ To cut flowing curves, turn the paper, not your scissors.

■ Stop cutting before you reach the tip of your scissors. Cutting with the tip can cause a little tear in the paper.

Make a Scissor Cut Scene

1. Draw a built-in frame.

2. Draw faces.

front view   side view

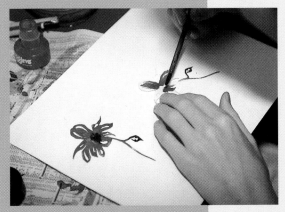

Colored inks make bright ▲
scissor cuts like these.
Watercolors are softer.

Paint Your Scissor Cuts

1. To paint your scissor cuts, spread them out on newspapers. Separate out the multiples now, or leave the stack together. The paint will seep through the layers.

2. Chinese papercuts often have details drawn with black ink. Before you paint, you may want to draw details with a permanent black pen.

3. Use watercolors or colored inks to paint your scissor cuts. Mix the colors you want to use. Test them on a scrap of paper and notice how they spread. Remember, the colors will dry lighter.

4. Use a brush to apply a small amount of color to one area at a time. Let the paper dry. Press the dry scissor cut under a book, or use a warm iron.

Mount Your Scissor Cuts

1. Cut a piece of heavy paper bigger than the scissor cut. Turn the scissor cut over. Use a toothpick to apply very small dots of glue down the center of the design. *(See diagram.)*

2. Line up your scissor cut in the center of the mounting paper. Gently press it in place. Lift up each side and apply more small dots of glue. Smooth the paper carefully from the center out. *(See diagram.)*

Mount Your Scissor Cuts

1-2. Mount the scissor cut.

glue

Other Ideas

■ Glue or tape a scissor cut to a window pane. Mount one in a clear plastic folder, and hang it in the window.

■ Mount small scissor cuts on the front of folded paper to make a card.

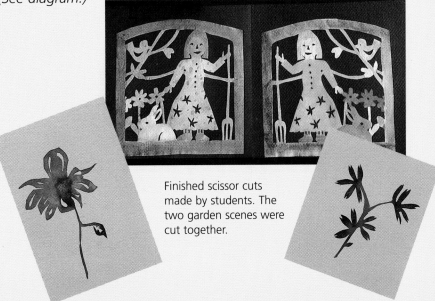

Finished scissor cuts made by students. The two garden scenes were cut together.

CHINA

RUSSIA

NORTH
KOREA

SOUTH
KOREA

SEA OF
JAPAN

Hokkaidō

● Sapporo

● Hakodate

● Akita

JAPAN

*PACIFIC
OCEAN*

*Oki
Island*

Honshū

Tokyo

*Mount
Fuji*

Nagoya ●

● Arimatsu

Kyōto ●

Hiroshima ●

Shikoku

Kitakyushu ●

Kochi ●

Kyūshū

Kagoshima ●

*EAST
CHINA
SEA*

*Ryukyu
Islands*

Okinawa

People come from all over the world to climb Mount Fuji.

In Japan there are religious shrines created especially for children.

These Tokyo children live in one of the biggest cities in the world.

Banraku puppet-makers are very respected artisans.

N
W   E
S

| 0 | | 200 miles |
| 0 | | 300 km |

Japan

▲ Tokyo's bullet train transports people at very high speeds.

Japan Facts

Name: Japan
Capital: Tokyo
Borders: East China Sea, Pacific Ocean, Sea of Japan
Nearest Neighbors: North Korea, South Korea, Russia, China
Size: 145,728 sq. mi. (377,803 sq km)
Population: 126 million
Language: Japanese
High/Low Point: Mount Fuji 12,389 ft. (3,776 m); sea level along the coast
Islands: 3,400 small islands; four major islands: Honshū, Hokkaidō, Kyūshū, Shikoku
Climate: Temperate with four seasons; temperatures range from 90° F (32° C) in Aug. to below 30° F (-1° C) in Jan.
Unusual Wildlife: Japanese black bear, snow monkey, giant salamander, white-cheeked flying squirrel, Japanese crane
Plants: At least 700 kinds of trees and shrubs; maple, cherry, pine, giant bamboo and bamboo undergrowth

High-Speed Tokyo

Packed into a crowded bullet train bound for Tokyo, visitors are quickly introduced to life in modern Japan. At speeds of over 168 miles (270 km) per hour, these high-speed trains whisk passengers to and from the world's most populated urban center. Millions of workers enter high-rise office buildings. Shoppers flock to areas like Ginza, one of Japan's most popular and expensive shopping districts.

Ancient Traditions and Modern Challenges

Within Tokyo's high-energy modern lifestyle there exists the quieter influence of Japan's traditional culture. Among tall office buildings are reminders of another age. Visitors can see older wooden houses, a kimono shop, and perhaps an old woman sweeping the pavement with a straw broom. On a clear winter day, Mount Fuji shows its snow-capped splendor to Tokyo's residents who, for centuries, have revered the beauty of nature. But nature is not always peaceful. Japan's many volcanoes, along with fires and earthquakes, have caused great hardships throughout history.

According to legend, Japan was created when brother and sister gods dipped a jeweled spear into the ocean and sprinkled saltwater drops down from the sky. These drops became the islands of Japan.

Most of Japan's 126 million people live on four small mountainous islands. Other people live on small islands scattered around the four larger ones. To understand Japan's population **density,** imagine one-half of the people in the United States living in an area the size of Montana. Conflicts and pressures from foreign powers have further challenged the Japanese people to unite and preserve their culture.

The Japanese people's respect for beauty, simplicity, and harmony help them to balance their fast-paced lives. These peaceful attitudes are reflected in Japanese arts and crafts. They are also preserved through art traditions, such as the shibori method of dyeing cloth.

◄ Japanese gardens are designed to give visitors inspiration and quiet.

▲ The Kiyomizu Temple in Kyōto is a center for the practice of Buddhism.

Shintoism and Buddhism

In Japan, religious beliefs and a respect for nature's beauty are closely connected. Almost every Japanese art form reflects the influence of Shintoism and Buddhism. These two ancient religions are still practiced today. Shintoism, which means "way of the gods," teaches that everything in nature has a spirit. It teaches people to live in harmony with nature and respect their ancestors.

Buddhism was brought to Japan in the 6th century by traveling Korean monks. A form of Buddhism called Zen teaches self-discipline and simplicity as a way to achieve a balance in mind, body, and spirit.

The Inspiration of Nature

The Japanese people have a deep love and respect for nature. Japan's blue seas, whispering pine trees, and high mountains have inspired Japanese artists for centuries. The Japanese people create miniature environments in their beautiful gardens. These carefully planned landscapes, containing trees, flowering shrubs, ponds, and streams, are true works of art.

Haiku poets, potters, painters, and shibori artists have all been inspired by nature's beauty. Poets like Bashō use words in their creations, while shibori artists use the colors and patterns of nature.

▲ Shinto shrines are found in beautiful natural settings, on top of department stores, and crowded between office buildings. They give people a place to experience a quiet moment in the midst of a busy day.

A Haiku Poem

On a withered branch
A crow is perched
An autumn evening.

Bashō (1644 – 1694)

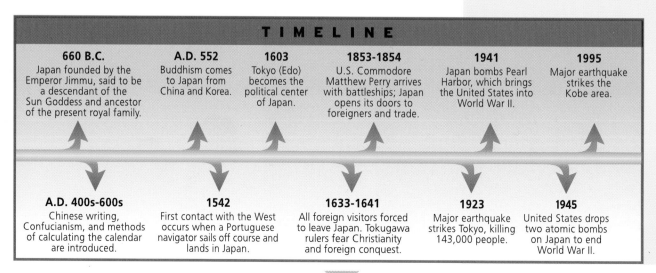

TIMELINE

660 B.C.
Japan founded by the Emperor Jimmu, said to be a descendant of the Sun Goddess and ancestor of the present royal family.

A.D. 552
Buddhism comes to Japan from China and Korea.

1603
Tokyo (Edo) becomes the political center of Japan.

1853-1854
U.S. Commodore Matthew Perry arrives with battleships; Japan opens its doors to foreigners and trade.

1941
Japan bombs Pearl Harbor, which brings the United States into World War II.

1995
Major earthquake strikes the Kobe area.

A.D. 400s-600s
Chinese writing, Confucianism, and methods of calculating the calendar are introduced.

1542
First contact with the West occurs when a Portuguese navigator sails off course and lands in Japan.

1633-1641
All foreign visitors forced to leave Japan. Tokugawa rulers fear Christianity and foreign conquest.

1923
Major earthquake strikes Tokyo, killing 143,000 people.

1945
United States drops two atomic bombs on Japan to end World War II.

Historic Traditions

Japan's contact with China began in the 5th century A.D. The Japanese people learned many things from the Chinese. They adopted Buddhism and a system of writing from the Chinese. They also learned how to weave silk.

The Japanese used what they learned to express their own beliefs and sense of beauty. They transformed, or changed, common objects and activities, including writing and the simple act of drinking tea, into beautiful and inspiring art forms.

Japanese Art Forms

weaving and dyeing

woodblock printing

tea ceremony

calligraphy

lacquerware

pottery

Haiku poetry

flower arranging

scroll painting

Kabuki theater

Noh theater

▲ The tea ceremony comes from Zen Buddhism. To make tea with the right spirit is a religious art that requires patience and training. All guests must bow low to enter a teahouse through a small door. This shows that, once they are inside, all people are equal.

The Beauty of Silk

Japan is one of the world's leading countries in producing silk. Silk, made from the cocoons of caterpillars called silkworms, is the strongest of all natural fibers. Many people think it is also the most beautiful. Silk is very lightweight, yet warm. Dyed silk has a deeper, richer appearance than most other dyed fabrics.

During the Edo Period (1614-1868), which really began in the 16th century, the ruling class would not allow common people to use silk for their clothing. After 1593, Japanese farmers began to grow cotton. By the end of the Edo Period, around 1868, yellow and white flowers of cotton plants could be seen all over Japan. Cotton was used to make shibori-decorated cloth for the **kimonos** of farmers and merchants. Today, kimonos are made from both cotton and silk.

◄ Japanese artists paint beautiful designs on fabric and paper.

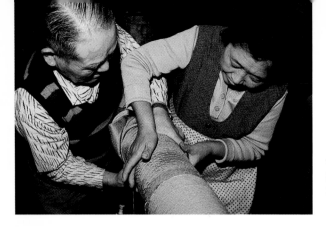

◄ Some artisans use the shibori tube-dyeing technique.

Kyōto

The ancient city of Kyōto has been the art center of Japan for hundreds of years. Cloth for beautiful Japanese traditional clothing is still produced there, using shibori and other methods.

Kyōto owes part of its importance in the Japanese **textile** industry to a river. The wide and very shallow Kamo River flows through the center of Kyōto. Its water is crystal clear. Nowhere else in Japan can fabrics be bleached so white and dyed in such beautiful and brilliant colors.

Arimatsu Village

Thousands of tourists visit Japan's famous Mount Fuji each year. Near this spectacular mountain is a small village tourists often overlook. For over 380 years, Arimatsu artisans have practiced the art of shibori.

During the Edo Period, textile craftsmen were sent to the Arimatsu area. They were assigned to work on textiles needed for the new Nagoya Castle. They stayed and built a shibori center in the area. Today, visitors can walk through Arimatsu. They can see the ancient houses where shibori artists worked and sold their cloth centuries ago. Modern shibori artists also work in their homes. They sell their cloth through a local **cooperative,** or group. Visitors can also see artists at work there.

Traditional Japanese homes like this one in Arimatsu have mat flooring. The size of the room is measured by the number of mats. The main room opens out to a garden. It usually has an altar space that holds special scrolls and flowers to fit the season. Furniture and tables are low to the floor, because people sit on cushions for dining. Shoes are always removed before entering the house.

◄ Arimatsu village has beautiful traditional homes that are centuries old.

The Japanese Kimono

Japan's early culture, including heavy, multi-layered clothing, was influenced by China. In particular, women's dress became very elaborate. An upper-class woman's clothing consisted of loose silk trousers worn under several silk robes of

▲ A mother and her daughters wear traditional clothing.

different colors. There were complicated rules about what a person could wear. A person's status in society could be told by the type and color of his or her clothing.

From the Ashikaga Period (1338-1573) to the Momoyama Period (1574-1600), the kimono became standard dress for both men and women. Its development into the national dress of Japan was one way the Japanese people developed their own distinctive styles and art forms despite foreign influences. The kimono was cut in a simple style as a long flowing robe, worn with a sash. Advances in weaving and dyeing techniques made it possible for artisans to produce beautiful and elegant kimonos. Fashion books from the Edo Period show the importance of intricate kimono designs to wealthy buyers.

Traditional Kimonos in Modern Japan

Visitors to Japan today see most people wearing Western-style clothing. However, handmade kimonos are still very much in demand. The Japanese people have a deep love for kimonos made with traditional techniques and designs. They wear kimonos designed for every season to reflect the beauty of nature.

Kimonos are worn as formal dress at ceremonies, parties, and weddings. Many art collectors purchase beautifully designed kimonos to exhibit.

Summer and Winter

Kimonos are made to a standard size, style, and cut. However, kimonos differ in color, pattern, and quality of fabric. Lined kimonos are worn in cool weather, and padded kimonos in winter. Winter sleeping kimonos, called *nemaki,* are made of warm flannel. Light and airy kimonos called *yukata* are worn in the summer.

Colored Lanterns

In Japan, people light lanterns and wear special clothing as a part of many festivals and ceremonies. They wear summer kimonos and dance to celebrate the spirits' visit. Buddhist temples glow in the warm light of colored lanterns.

◀ Arimatsu women work together to tie the cloth for dyeing.

The Art of Decorated Cloth

Since ancient times, Japanese people of wealth and power liked clothing made from colorful and richly designed silk fabric. Even ordinary clothing used by common people was made of beautifully dyed cotton. As a result, the art of weaving and dyeing cloth became very important. Many methods for producing beautiful cloth and designs were created, including shibori dyeing and **embroidery.**

Shibori Dyeing

The shibori technique, or method, of tying and dyeing cloth is the oldest of many decorative crafts. It began in the 700s, during the time of Chinese influence. Small portions of fabric are gathered and tied with thread in a particular design. Only those parts are dipped into pots of boiling dye. Because the thread is tightly wound, the color cannot reach the fabric beyond it, leaving only the gathered part colored. Multicolored patterns are made using this process.

Sometimes, several artists work together to make one large piece of cloth using various designs and methods. One piece of decorated cloth with a complex pattern could take over 300 hours to produce.

Dyed cloth from Kyōto is ▶ famous for its vibrant colors.

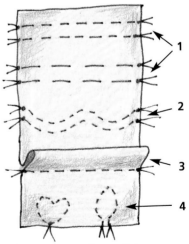

Have fun exploring different Japanese shibori dyeing techniques. Then combine the patterns to create a beautiful and unique cushion cover.

Tools

- scissors
- embroidery needle
- galvanized or stainless steel dye pot
- smock or apron
- rubber gloves
- dust mask
- long-handled spoon
- old towel

Materials

- white 100% cotton muslin or lightweight sheeting, prewashed to remove fabric stiffeners
- heavy carpet thread
- colored chalk
- all-purpose dyes that need heating
- non-iodized salt, available in grocery stores
- 3 in. (7 cm) foam cushion, 18 in. by 18 in. (46 by 46 cm)

Experiment with *Shibori*

Stitching and binding are two shibori techniques. Special stitches and knots keep the dye from soaking through and leave a pattern on the fabric. Experiment on 12-inch (30 cm) squares of white cotton before you start your final project. Try different methods, and then dye your test pieces all together. Make them into napkins or small pillows if you want.

Shibori Stitching

1. Thread a needle with a piece of carpet thread, or other very strong thread, about 3-feet (90-cm) long. Double the thread. Tie a large knot at the end. Sew across the fabric using a *running stitch*. (See page 15.) When you reach the edge, cut the needle off of the thread. Leave two short tails of thread hanging loose at the end. *(See diagram.)*

2. Thread the needle again. Try some of the stitching variations listed here. Don't allow the rows of stitches to cross each other.

Shibori Stitching

1. Sew across the fabric with a *running stitch*.

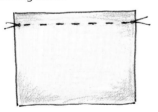

Experiment with stitching. ▶

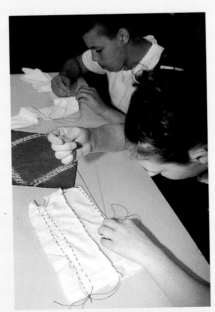

Stitching Variations

1. Use short or long stitches.

2. Practice stitching curved lines.

3. Fold the fabric in half and stitch along the edge.

4. Stitch around the outline of a simple shape, such as a heart or leaf.

3. When the test piece is full of stitches, pull the threads up tightly. Hold on to the loose ends of the threads. Slide the fabric toward the knotted ends into a tight gather. The tighter you pull the threads, the clearer your pattern will be. *(See diagram.)*

4. Tie the loose ends with a *square knot.* Put the right thread over the left. Then put the left over the right, as shown. Pull tight. This will hold the bunched fabric in place. Repeat for each row of stitches. Put the test piece aside until you are ready to dye the fabric. *(See diagram.)*

Shibori Binding

Now experiment with binding. First, learn to make a *kamosage knot.* This is a special slip knot that will stay tight while you dye the fabric.

1. Cut a piece of heavy thread about 2 feet (60 cm) long. On a new piece of muslin, pull a little tuft of fabric straight up. Don't twist it. Hold the tuft and one end of the thread in one hand.

2. With the other hand, wrap the thread clockwise four times around the tuft, very tightly. Tuck the short end of the thread securely under the wrapping. *(See diagram.)*

3. Continue to hold the wrapped tuft so that it stays tight. With your other hand, make a loop around your fingers, as shown. Press the thread under your thumb against your third finger. Spread your first two fingers apart. *(See diagram.)*

4. Pull the cloth around to the front of the loop. Slip the tuft under the loop and up. Slide the loop slowly, closing it around the tuft. You've made a *kamosage knot!* Pull the knot tight. The wrapped tuft will become a white ring on the dyed fabric. *(See diagram.)*

5. Bind several tufts in a row without cutting the thread. Stretch the long end of the thread over to each new tuft. Try some of the variations shown on page 43.

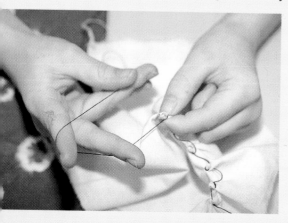

◄ When making more than one *kamosage knot,* stretch the long end of the thread over to each new tuft.

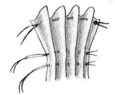

3. Pull the threads up tightly.

4. Tie a square knot.

Shibori Binding

2. Wrap the thread four times tightly.

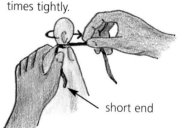

short end

3. Make the loop around your fingers.

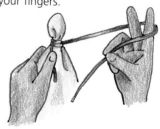

4. Slip the tuft under the loop, and up.

Binding Variations

■ Wrap the thread in a wide band for thicker ring.

■ Space the turns of the thread so that some cloth is exposed to make a spiral design.

■ Bind a row of rings to outline a simple shape.

■ Fill a shape with rings.

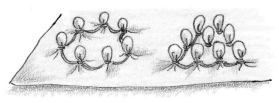

Dye Safety

■ Make sure an adult is present when you are dyeing.

■ Dyes will stain clothes, tables, floors, and skin. Cover every surface with plastic. Wear an apron to protect your clothes. Wear rubber gloves to protect your hands.

■ Dye powders can be harmful if inhaled. Wear a dust mask until the powder is dissolved in water.

■ Do not use the dye pot or mixing containers for food. Thoroughly wash dye out of the sink.

Dye the Fabric

4. Remove the stitches and the knots.

cut

Dye the Fabric

Now you are ready to dye your small test pieces. Traditional colors for this fabric are blue, purple, and red. In Japan, natural dyes are used, but synthetic all-purpose dyes are easier to use. Choose any color that you like. Follow the dye safety guidelines. **Have an adult help you all through the dyeing process.**

1. Follow the instructions on the dye package very carefully. All-purpose dyes need to be heated to make the color dark. Fill the dye pot with one gallon (4 liters) of water.

2. Dissolve the dye with a little hot water in a plastic container. Add this to the dye pot. Add salt also, if it isn't already mixed in with the dye. Salt helps to fix the dye chemically to the fabric.

3. Soak the test squares in a tub of clear water for five minutes. Wet fabric will soak up dye more evenly than dry fabric. When the dye and salt are dissolved, add the fabric to the pot. Heat the water to just below boiling. Keep it bubbling gently for the recommended time. Stir the fabric often.

4. After dyeing, rinse the fabric until the water runs clear. Lay the wet test squares on an old towel to dry. When dry, you can remove the stitches and knots. Cut the stitched threads carefully to avoid making holes. To remove the *kamosage knot,* pull on the edges of the fabric. The knots will slip off the top of the tufts. Wash the test squares separately, and dry. *(See diagram.)*

Pull the edges of the fabric, and ▶ the knots will slip off the tufts.

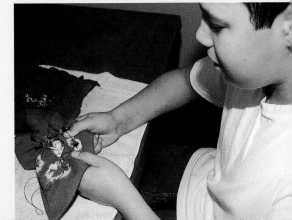

Plan a *Shibori* Floor Cushion

Stitching and binding methods can be used to make many traditional Japanese patterns. Several are described and illustrated here. Study these patterns and your test squares to get ideas. Draw a plan for your cushion. You can plan patterns for both sides or just for the top.

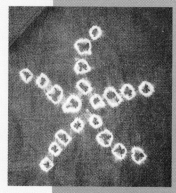

▲ The starfish pattern.

Stitched Patterns

■ **wood grain** – Sew close, parallel rows of *running stitches* to fill an area.

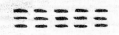

■ **meandering (wandering) stream** – Sew three or more rows of stitches in flowing curves to fill an area.

■ **pinecone** – Stitch three small half circles within one another along the edge of a fold.

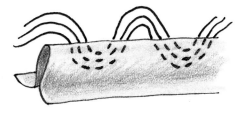

Bound Patterns

■ **starfish** – Bind rings in the shape of a starfish. Form the center with five rings and the legs with gradually smaller rings.

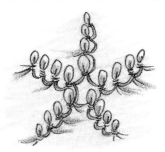

■ **shell** – Wrap a tuft of cloth from the base to the top, spacing the turns of the thread so that some cloth is exposed. Tie a *kamosage knot* at the top. This will create a delicate spiral design.

Combination Patterns

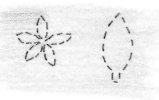

■ **cherry blossom** – Sew around the outline of a simple five-petaled flower. Pull the stitches tight and tie the ends. Draw the center of the flower up into a tuft and bind a ring around it.

■ **leaf** – Sew around the outline of a leaf shape. Pull the stitches tight. Pull the inside of the leaf up into a tuft. Wrap the end of the stitching thread from the base to the top, spacing the turns as in a shell pattern. Tie a *kamosage knot*.

◄ The pinecone pattern becomes a circle when the fold is opened.

Make a *Shibori* Floor Cushion

1. Measure the fabric.

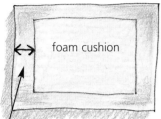

foam cushion

extra for sides and seam

2. Mark the patterns with chalk.

5. Sew the cushion pieces together.

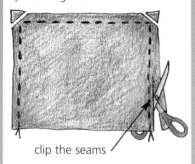

clip the seams

Other Ideas

■ Plan a two-color project. Leave knots and stitches in place after the first dye bath. Add more knots and stitches. Dye the second color.

Make a *Shibori* Floor Cushion

1. Measure two pieces of fabric for the front and back of the cushion. Make each piece four inches (10 cm) wider and four inches (10 cm) longer than your foam cushion to allow for the sides and seam. *(See diagram.)*

2. Cut and iron the fabric. Spread it out on a table. Use colored chalk to mark the locations of the shibori patterns you have planned. *(See diagram.)*

3. Sew all the stitched patterns first. Cut the thread ends and leave them hanging. Don't gather them yet, or it will be hard to work on the other patterns. Next, tie the bound patterns. Last, gather the threads of the stitches and tie them off.

4. Dye the cushion fabric just as you dyed the test pieces. Rinse well, dry, and remove the stitches and knots. Wash, dry, and iron the fabric.

5. Pin the two cushion pieces together and sew around three edges. Clip the seams as shown and turn them to the inside. Insert the foam cushion and sew the final edge closed. *(See diagram.)*

◄ Three cushions dyed by students.

Glossary

artisans people who are skilled in an art, a craft, or a trade

cooperative a group formed in order to successfully produce and sell a product, such as handicrafts

density in population, the average number of people in a given space

dynasties powerful families that rule a country generation after generation

embroidery decorative needlework

exaggerated oversized, out of proportion, or overstated

grotesque a presentation of something natural, like a human face, that makes it look ugly and exaggerated

Haiku poem, often about the seasons, that contains 17 syllables

kimono a traditional, brightly colored, robelike Japanese garment

literacy the ability to read and write; a skill that is needed in a country where people elect leaders and determine their own future

monsoons seasonal weather characterized by very heavy rainfall

nomads herders who migrate, or move, with their animals according to the season

peninsula a piece of land nearly surrounded by water

ravine small, narrow, steep-sided valley

sparsely thinly distributed or widely spread

steppe a large, semidry, grass-covered plateau, or plain

supernatural appearing to be beyond what is normal or able to be explained by the laws of nature

template pattern

textile hand-woven or machine-knitted cloth

yurts tents made of felt; today many yurts are covered with canvas

Abbreviation Key

C	Centigrade
cm	centimeters
F	Fahrenheit
ft.	feet
g	grams
in.	inches
km	kilometers
m	meters
mi.	miles
ml	milliliters
oz.	ounces
sq.	square
yd.	yards

Resources

Mongolia

Hull, Mary. *The Mongol Empire,* "World History" series. San Diego, CA: Lucent, 1997
Humphrey, Judy. *Genghis Khan,* "World Leaders—Past and Present" series. Broomall, PA: Chelsea House, 1987
Sjöberg, Gunilla Paetau. *Felt: New Directions for an Ancient Craft.* Loveland, CO: Interweave Press, 1996
Wilson, Diane Lee. *I Rode a Horse of Milk White Jade.* New York: Orchard, 1998

Korea

Adams, Edward B. *Korean Folk Art and Craft.* Seoul: Seoul International Publishing House, 1987
Choi, Sook Nyul. *Echoes of the White Giraffe.* Boston, MA: Houghton Miffin, 1993
Hunter, Ruth S. *A Part of the Ribbon: A Time Travel Adventure Through the History of Korea.* New York: Turtle Press, 1997
Jung, Song-Hoon. *South Korea,* "Economically Developing Countries" series. Austin, TX: Raintree Steck-Vaughn, 1997
McMahon, Patricia. *Chi-Hoon, a Korean Girl.* Honesdale, PA: Boyds Mills, 1993

Japan

Barton, J., M.K. Rice, and Y. Wada. *Shibori: The Inventive Art of Japanese Shaped Resist Dyeing: Tradition, Techniques, Innovation.* Tokyo: Kodansha International Ltd., 1983

Downer, Lesley. *Japan,* "Modern Industrial World" series. Austin, TX: Raintree Steck-Vaughn, 1995

Meyer, Carolyn. *A Voice from Japan: An Outsider Looks In.* New York: Harcourt Brace, 1992

Ross, Stewart. *Rise of Japan and the Pacific Rim,* "Causes and Consequences" series. Austin, TX: Raintree Steck-Vaughn, 1995

China

Baldwin, Robert F. *Daily Life in Ancient and Modern Beijing,* "Cities Through Time" series. Minneapolis, MN: Lerner, 1999

Borja, Robert, and Corinne Borja. *Making Chinese Papercuts.* Morton Grove, IL: Albert Whitman, 1980

Charley, Catherine. *China,* "Country Fact Files" series. Austin, TX: Raintree Steck-Vaughn, 1995

Waterlow, Julia. *China,* "Economically Developing Countries" series. Austin, TX: Raintree Steck-Vaughn, 1995

Index

Acknowledgments

Special thanks to these students for their time and energy in making the project samples: Anna, Brian, Carrie B., Carrie S., Eleanor, Jeff, Laurel, Naomi, Samantha W., and Tim; and to Aisha, Arias, Louis, and Samantha Z. for their help. Thanks also to Jefferson Middle School, Eugene, Oregon; Christie Newland; Daphne Stone; Diane Cissel, Terragraphics; Stephen Reynolds; Libris Solar; City Copy; Percy Franklin; and Wade Long. Special thanks to Gary Tepfer for his ongoing support of this project, to Elaine Faris Keenan for making available her photo library of Japanese folk art and artisans, and to the Korean Overseas Information Service and the Korean Cultural Center of Los Angeles.